MENSA®

SUPER-SMART

MIND
TWISTERS

MENSA®

SUPER-SMART

MIND TWISTERS

—112—

WORD, LOGIC, NUMBER,
AND REASONING PUZZLES

DAVID MILLAR
WITH AMERICAN MENSA

Skyhorse Publishing

Skyhorse Publishing books may be purchased in bulk at special discounts for sales promotion, corporate gifts, fund-raising, or educational purposes. Special editions can also be created to specifications. For details, contact the Special Sales Department, Skyhorse Publishing, 307 West 36th Street, 11th Floor, New York, NY 10018 or info@skyhorsepublishing.com.

Skyhorse® and Skyhorse Publishing® are registered trademarks of Skyhorse Publishing, Inc.®, a Delaware corporation.

Visit our website at www.skyhorsepublishing.com.

10 9 8 7 6 5 4 3 2 1

Library of Congress Cataloging-in-Publication Data is available on file.

Cover design by Brian Peterson and David Ter-Avanesyan
Cover illustration by David Millar

Print ISBN: 978-1-5107-6683-9

Printed in China

Contents

Puzzles

Throwing Shade 1

Shade some cells so the remaining letters in each row and column spell answers to the provided clues. Clues are sorted alphabetically by answer.

M	R	I	S	O	W	S	D	Y
O	Y	C	C	A	A	T	R	E
P	E	S	L	O	T	S	O	T
R	A	C	O	R	U	T	S	A
E	S	A	R	H	C	O	P	S
O	T	L	E	A	H	O	P	S
I	C	H	E	E	E	S	S	E
S	C	L	R	O	E	C	S	T
C	H	E	E	S	L	E	R	C

Rows

- Part of the heart
- Curved shape
- Give attention
- Dairy product
- Jumps
- Frozen material
- Misplaced
- Mix of nuts and greens
- Wild

Columns

- Central part
- Bits of rain
- Iconic sandwich cookies
- Image
- Grabbing distance
- Shopping event
- Part of the foot
- Wrist accessory
- Bread ingredient

Tetra Grid 1

Drop each of the shapes into the grid in the order provided to spell ten six-letter words. Clues for the words have been provided next to the grid.

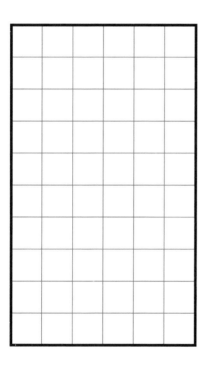

Judge

Gross and offensive

Purpose

Alright

Prop gun ammunition

Coastal city

Split

Melted fat

Card game participant

Count

Rearrangement 1–2

Rearrange the letters in the phrase "SCRIPTED JOY" to spell some delightful features on home improvement shows.

Rearrange the letters in the phrase "TACKY TROPICAL" to spell an event where one might find some tropical drinks with little umbrellas.

Story Logic 1

An indie wrestling company is planning a string of big shows for next spring and summer. Use the clues to match the month of the event with the host city and the good and bad guy in the main event match.

		Host City				Good Guy				Bad Guy			
		Abilene	Denton	Mineral Wells	Waco	Cowboy Carter	Danny B	Easy Gary Easton	Fly Frank Smith	Quick Shot Sal	Randy Willis	Smooth Stunta	Terrible Terry
Month	February												
	April												
	June												
	August												
Bad Guy	Quick Shot Sal												
	Randy Willis												
	Smooth Stunta												
	Terrible Terry												
Good Guy	Cowboy Carter												
	Danny B												
	Easy Gary Easton												
	Fly Frank Smith												

Cowboy Carter and Terrible Terry face off in a main event sometime before the event in Mineral Wells.

Randy Willis is not main eventing in Denton, nor is his main event match with Danny B.

Quick Shot Sal's main event match is with either Danny B or Easy Gary Easton, and comes before the event being held in Waco.

The event in Abilene will be held in August, but its main event does not feature Randy Willis.

The show where Danny B is in the main event will take place at the next event held after the one in Denton.

Fly Frank Smith will not be competing against Smooth Stunta when he has his main event match.

Kakuro 1

Fill the grid with digits 1 through 9 so that each continuous section of row or column contains no repeated digits, and sums to the total provided at the top or left of the section.

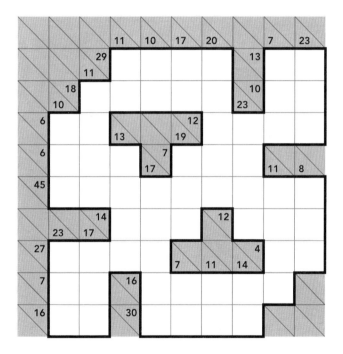

Numcross 1

Use the provided clues to fill the grid with numbers. No entry may start with a 0.

A	B	C		D	E
F				G	
		H	I		
J	K				
L			M	N	O
P			Q		

Across

A. K down - 80
D. O down × 3
F. A down × 2
G. L across - 9
H. D across × E down
J. Even digits that sum to B down
L. A down - 2
M. A perfect square
P. D down / N down
Q. L across × 3

Down

A. Another perfect square
B. J down / O down
C. H across + E down
D. A palindrome
E. Entry-level course number
I. One-half of J across
J. A palindrome
K. A across + 80
N. O down + 6
O. Sum of the digits in D down

Symbol Sums 1

The sums of five combinations of symbols have been provided. What is the value of each individual symbol?

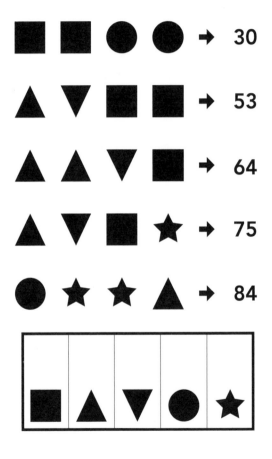

Transit Map 1

Use the clues to fill the bus route with letters to form words both northbound and southbound.

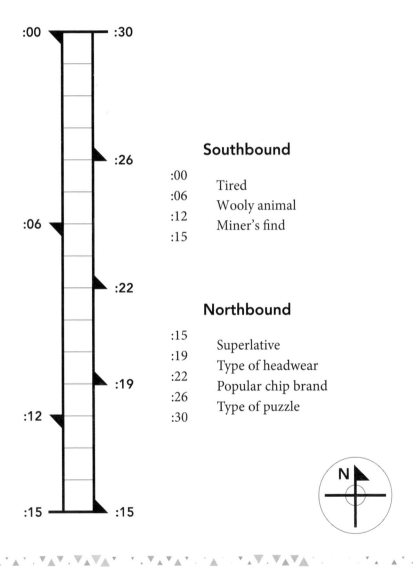

Southbound

:00
:06   Tired
:12   Wooly animal
:15   Miner's find

Northbound

:15
:19   Superlative
:22   Type of headwear
:26   Popular chip brand
:30   Type of puzzle

Cube Logic 1

Which of the four foldable patterns can be folded to make the cube displayed?

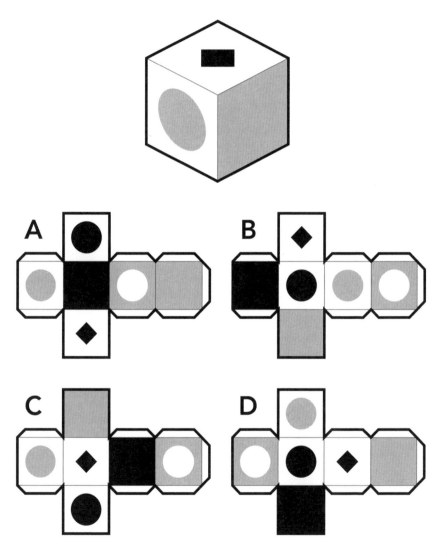

In Memoriam 1A

Memorize the words shown in the list below. When you're ready, turn the page and put your memory to the test.

Boat

Coast

Grout

Hours

Loan

Lounge

Moat

Proof

Routine

Stout

Trousers

In Memoriam 1B

Moving up, down, left, and right, make a path from Start to Finish. You may only pass through squares that contain words from the list on the previous page.

S	Loan	Trousers	Grout	Bored
Boat	Sport	Block	Tornado	Posh
Stout	Rosy	Globe	Cover	Lost
Routine	Womb	Lounge	Proof	Hours
Coast	Proof	Moat	Post	F

Word Search

Find the words in the list below. They're somewhere in the book. (Somewhere besides the list, I mean.)

Celebrated

Delectable

Electrical

Enchiladas

Essentials

Flashlight

Streamline

Sweatshirt

Traditions

Throwing Shade 2

Shade some cells so the remaining letters in each row and column spell answers to the provided clues. Clues are sorted alphabetically by answer.

T	B	S	H	O	P	B	S	T
S	B	T	O	R	A	E	S	T
T	T	H	W	H	A	O	P	R
B	L	H	E	E	O	A	P	T
P	E	R	R	I	C	I	S	M
O	D	E	I	N	T	W	O	E
P	A	U	I	N	T	T	Y	R
I	J	U	N	K	M	N	P	E
C	U	B	N	B	T	K	Y	E

Rows

- Type of mammal
- Blocky object
- Musician Clapton
- Printer necessity
- Get off the ground
- Age of a baby, perhaps
- Sculptor's material
- Mall contents
- Hammer-wielding god

Columns

- Cheese variety
- Farm animal
- Breakfast grain
- Pig noise
- Agreement
- Hedge
- Covert operative
- Subject
- Woody plant

Rearrangement 3–4

Rearrange the letters in the phrase "IRONICALLY A FOOD HOWL" to spell a place where an actor portraying a hungry werewolf might be seen.

Rearrange the letters in the phrase "ANGELIC FINS" to spell some items that bring heavenly relief during a heat wave.

Tetra Grid 2

Drop each of the shapes into the grid in the order provided to spell ten six-letter words. Clues for the words have been provided next to the grid.

Cause change

Beverage sampler

Tent user

Assigned

Place of memorial/dedication

Something drawn?

Painting style

Plans

Google's web browser

Open-roofed court

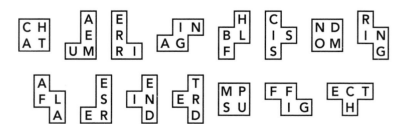

Numcross 2

Use the provided clues to fill the grid with numbers. No entry may start with a 0.

A	B		C	D	E
F			G		
H		I			
		J		K	L
M	N			O	
P				Q	

Across

A. One-half of O across

C. Fake telephone number prefix

F. O across - 1

G. Consecutive digits in ascending order

H. A power of two

J. Digits that sum to N down

M. D down + F across

O. A across × 2

P. Digits that sum to one-fifth of O across

Q. A perfect cube

Down

A. Digits that multiply to M down

B. A across + C across

C. I down × 2

D. A across in reverse

E. Q across × 2

I. Digits that sum to a total of 13

K. E down × M down

L. F across × 3

M. One-third of E down

N. Q across - 4

Rows Garden 1

Using the clues provided, enter a letter into each triangle to fill the garden. Each row contains one or two entries, and each hexagonal flower contains a six-letter word wrapped around the center. It's up to you to determine where to place the starting letter and the direction of the word.

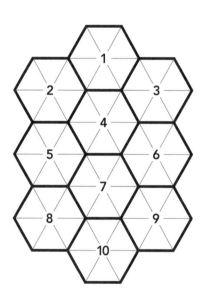

80's TV alien

"Great job!"/Classic phone noise

Oft-juiced fruit/Craft marketplace

Ahead of schedule/Cooking fat

Famous on the web/Insects

Casino object/Seething

Worthy of mention/Untamed

Airport checkpoint folks

Flowers

1. Candy attribute
2. Heat-retaining stone
3. Greedy
4. Isolated feeling
5. Show up

6. Some bank employees
7. Pre-wedding shower
8. Egg packaging
9. Clean meticulously
10. Used poorly

Kakuro 2

Fill the grid with digits 1 through 9 so that each continuous section of row or column contains no repeated digits, and sums to the total provided at the top or left of the section.

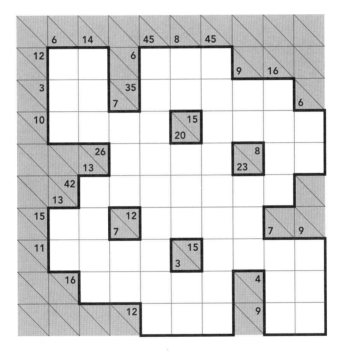

Symbol Sums 2

The sums of five combinations of symbols have been provided. What is the value of each individual symbol?

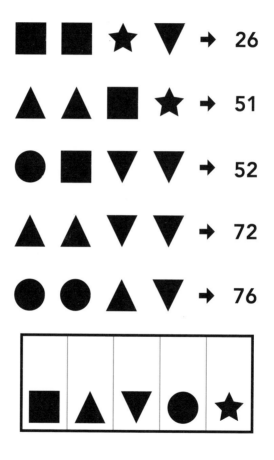

Transit Map 2

Use the clues to fill the bus route with letters to form words both northbound and southbound.

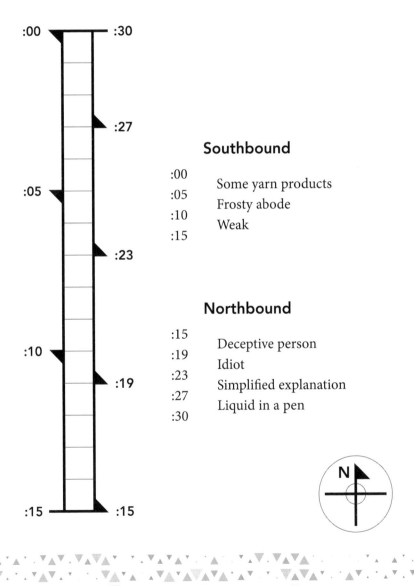

Southbound

:00
:05   Some yarn products
:10   Frosty abode
:15   Weak

Northbound

:15
:19   Deceptive person
:23   Idiot
:27   Simplified explanation
:30   Liquid in a pen

Cube Logic 2

Which of the four foldable patterns can be folded to make the cube displayed?

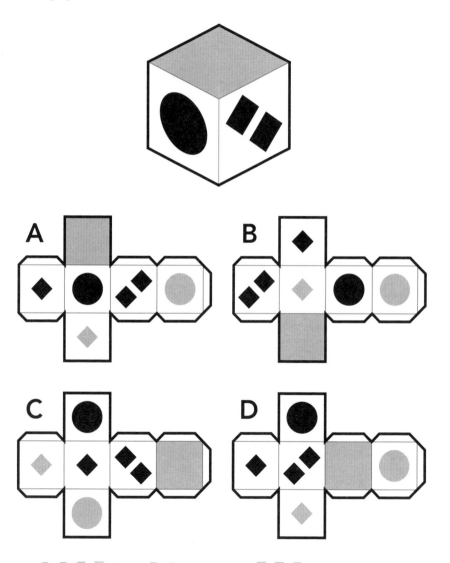

Rebus Deli 1–2

What tasty morsels are clued by the pictures?

___

GREEN
I
S

Tetra Grid 3

Drop each of the shapes into the grid in the order provided to spell ten six-letter words. Clues for the words have been provided next to the grid.

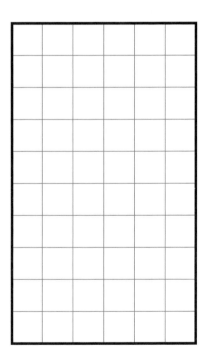

Go back

Between-meal food

Winter formation

Make smaller

A state of matter

Miniature sandwich

Royal abode

Stupidity

Courtroom occupant

Out for the night

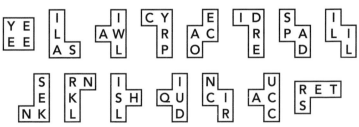

Numcross 3

Use the provided clues to fill the grid with numbers. No entry may start with a 0.

A	B	C		D	E
F				G	
		H	I		
J	K				
L			M	N	O
P			Q		

Across

A. Consecutive digits not in order

D. B down - 5

F. A multiple of B down

G. Consecutive digits in ascending order

H. J across - N down

J. Odd digits that sum to B down

L. Days (or weeks) in zombie film series titles

M. A down × D across

P. A perfect square

Q. A down × O down

Down

A. Halloween's day in Oct.

B. Another perfect square

C. Year President Obama's second term began

D. O down squared

E. B down + D down

I. Consecutive digits not in order

J. A down × 4

K. Consecutive digits in ascending order

N. Length of the Biblical flood in days

O. A down in reverse

Symbol Sums 3

The sums of five combinations of symbols have been provided.
What is the value of each individual symbol?

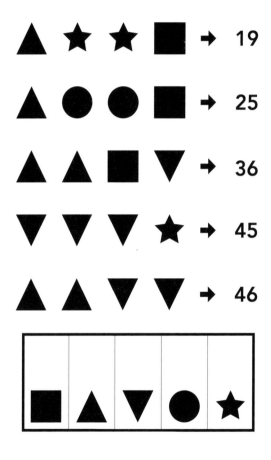

Throwing Shade 3

Shade some cells so the remaining letters in each row and column spell answers to the provided clues. Clues are sorted alphabetically by answer.

S	A	A	L	C	A	V	E	E
T	A	N	A	C	H	O	C	S
D	R	B	P	R	H	I	L	E
A	B	E	R	U	B	I	I	A
C	H	E	M	A	D	D	A	R
T	A	O	E	W	E	L	M	R
U	B	G	O	L	U	D	Y	A
E	L	L	Y	E	L	N	E	N
U	E	G	E	L	L	Y	B	N

Rows

- Scandinavian band
- Cheese variety
- Sea dweller
- Daytime talk host
- Angry
- Medical paste
- Tex-Mex staple
- Tall structure
- Looking bad

Columns

- Fit to do so
- Clocktower feature
- Stagnant body of water
- Move like a baby
- Gain through work
- Part of the face
- Uncool
- 3D art piece
- Cancel

Story Logic 2

Five drivers left their cars at the repair shop for service this morning. Use the notes on the adjacent page to match the vehicle to the needed service and the customer that needs to be called when their vehicle is ready.

		Service					Vehicle				
		AC Diagnostic	Brake Repair	Oil Change	Replace Battery	Tire Rotation	Blue Car	Blue SUV	Green Van	Red SUV	Yellow Car
Customer	Linda										
	Mark										
	Neisha										
	Olly										
	Pal										
Vehicle	Blue Car										
	Blue SUV										
	Green Van										
	Red SUV										
	Yellow Car										

One of the cars (as opposed to SUVs or vans) has AC problems. The other needs its brakes repaired.

The red vehicle is the one that needed its battery replaced.

Pal's van does not need its tires rotated.

Mark and Olly had the vehicles that needed tire rotation and AC service in some order.

Neisha's SUV needs either its battery replaced or an oil change.

Linda and Mark both have blue vehicles.

Kakuro 3

Fill the grid with digits 1 through 9 so that each continuous section of row or column contains no repeated digits, and sums to the total provided at the top or left of the section.

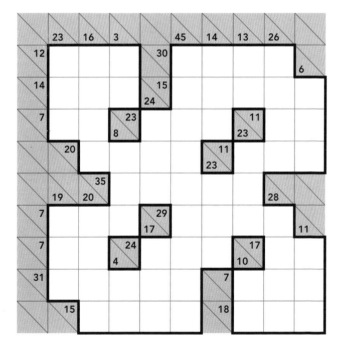

Rearrangement 5–6

Rearrange the letters in the phrase "DESPISE WHIRLWIND" to spell an automobile feature that helps in stormy weather.

Rearrange the letters in the phrase "GUTTER PROCESSOR" to spell items that keep computer equipment from becoming damaged.

Numcross 4

Use the provided clues to fill the grid with numbers. No entry may start with a 0.

A	B		C	D	E
F			G		
H		I			
		J		K	L
M	N			O	
P				Q	

Across

A. A perfect square

C. F across squared

F. Forms a full set of all ten digits with A, C, and G across

G. Sum of all the digits in a standard 9x9 sudoku

H. P across × Q across

J. F across + H across

M. A palindrome

O. M down × 2

P. E down + 6

Q. F across + 1

Down

A. C across + O across

B. Consecutive digits in ascending order

C. A down × 8

D. N down - 10

E. D down + the sum of the digits from L down

I. M down × P across

K. Consecutive digits in descending order

L. Digits multiply to D down

M. Sum of the digits in M across

N. Q across × 5

In Memoriam 2A

Memorize the words shown in the list below. When you're ready,
turn the page and put your memory to the test.

Man

Plan

Winner

Chicken

Dinner

Thicken

Beginner

Fine

Wine

Dine

Mine

In Memoriam 2B

Moving up, down, left, and right, make a path from Start to Finish. You may only pass through squares that DO NOT contain words from the list on the previous page.

S	Dinner	Bind	Winner	Wine
Sinner	Line	Kind	Chicken	Thicken
Sign	Mine	Find	Spinner	Sicken
Man	Flan	Plan	Sine	Dine
Fine	Can	Span	Pine	**F**

Tetra Grid 4

Drop each of the shapes into the grid in the order provided to spell ten six-letter words. Clues for the words have been provided next to the grid.

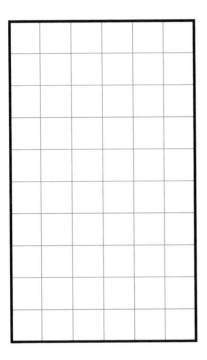

Snackable nut

Road marking

Wedding place

Worship place

Collage

Barely perceptible

Yellow fruit

Musical effect

Unpaved road surface

Cord adapter

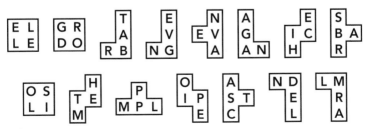

Transit Map 3

Use the clues to fill the bus route with letters to form words both northbound and southbound.

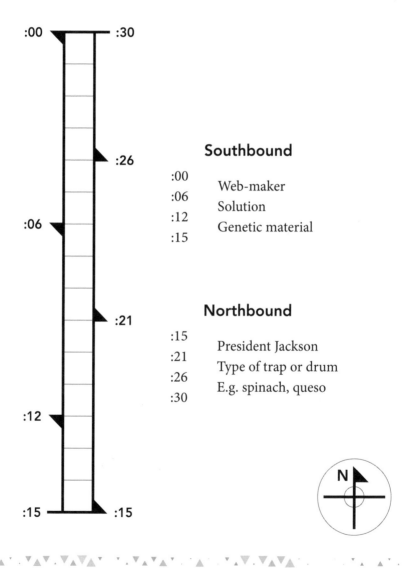

Southbound

:00
:06   Web-maker
:12   Solution
:15   Genetic material

Northbound

:15
:21   President Jackson
:26   Type of trap or drum
:30   E.g. spinach, queso

Cube Logic 3

Which of the four foldable patterns can be folded to make the cube displayed?

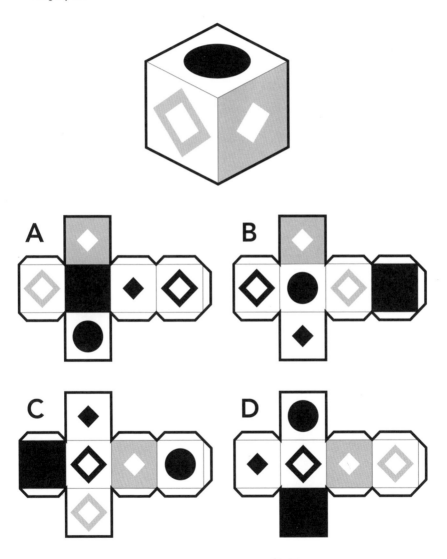

Rebus Deli 3–4

What tasty morsels are clued by the pictures?

MEATBALL

LEM
ADE

Rows Garden 2

Using the clues provided, enter a letter into each triangle to fill the garden. Each row contains one or two entries, and each hexagonal flower contains a six-letter word wrapped around the center. It's up to you to determine where to place the starting letter and the direction of the word.

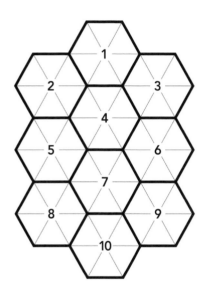

Big primate

Singing group/Travelled on

A deadly sin/Another deadly sin

Card below ace/More up-to-date

Senior/Weather factor

Auto brand/Mani-pedi focus

The rest

Zone encompassing west coast

Flowers

1. Fix

2. Educational institution

3. Removed

4. Measure as with a ruler

5. eBook device

6. Go back

7. Move about aimlessly

8. Previous

9. Little burger

10. Artist materials

Throwing Shade 4

Shade some cells so the remaining letters in each row and column spell answers to the provided clues. Clues are sorted alphabetically by answer.

N	D	O	U	T	S	L	A	H
S	O	R	N	A	G	E	O	B
E	A	T	D	E	I	L	L	I
V	I	U	B	E	O	R	W	A
T	T	W	A	X	A	I	M	I
A	S	E	N	A	P	G	O	T
D	K	E	C	Y	Y	G	N	S
A	M	R	C	B	C	H	E	R
B	I	K	E	S	T	T	D	T

Rows

- Throb with pain
- Greatest
- Potential lunch location
- Chewy, fruity candy
- Midwestern state
- Items on a ring
- Perform a theft
- Catch
- Lyft competitor

Columns

- Favoritism
- Awkward school event
- CD predecessor
- First day creation
- Miners' find
- Be indebted to
- Vegan "milk" source
- Web browser item
- Large US state

Sudoku Bites 1–2

In these two sudoku bites, fill each row, column, and thick-outlined rectangle with one of each digit 1 through 6. The digits along the arrows must add up to the digit in the attached circle.

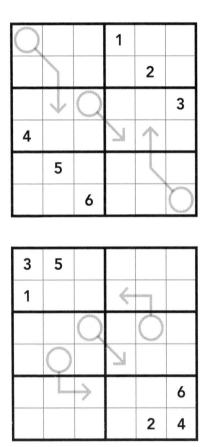

Rearrangement 7–8

Rearrange the letters in the phrase "UPBEAT TOT ETHOS" to spell something a small, overexcitable child can use to make a minty mess.

Rearrange the letters in the phrase "MINUS BEARS" to spell places you might go to spot sharks, fish, and whales, but not bears.

Numcross 5

Use the provided clues to fill the grid with numbers. No entry may start with a 0.

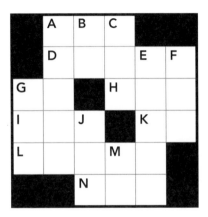

Across

A. G down + 39

D. An anagram of E down

G. A perfect square

H. G across + K across

I. Digits that sum to a multiple of 7

K. Problems enumerated in a Jay-Z song

L. Two digits forming a full house

N. F down in reverse

Down

A. Consecutive digits not in order

B. A perfect cube

C. A palindrome that is one-fifth of N across

E. Contains one of each odd digit

F. E down / M down

G. C down × 2

J. H across - 6

M. Another perfect square

Symbol Sums 4

The sums of five combinations of symbols have been provided.
What is the value of each individual symbol?

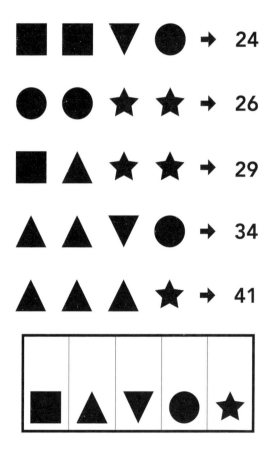

In Memoriam 3A

Memorize the shapes shown in the grid below. When you're ready, turn the page and put your memory to the test.

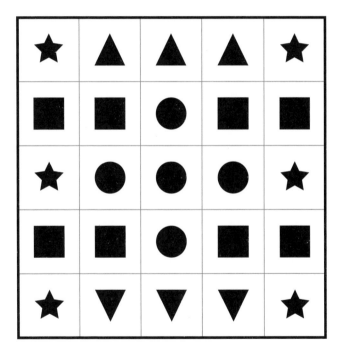

In Memoriam 3B

In the grid below, find the one row or column whose shapes are all the same as the shapes in the same position on the previous page.

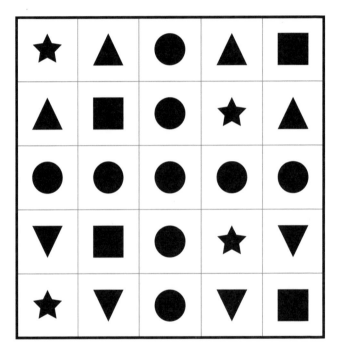

Tetra Grid 5

Drop each of the shapes into the grid in the order provided to spell ten six-letter words. Clues for the words have been provided next to the grid.

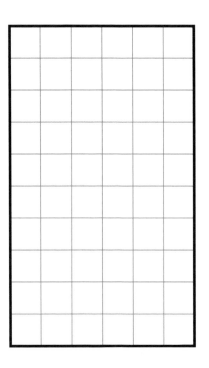

Hit

Compliment

First voyage

Suitable to eat

Bite gently

Horse shelter

Made coins

Batches of eggs

Like a zombie

Small landmass

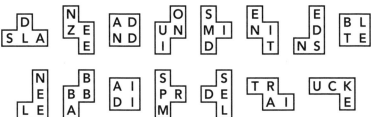

Story Logic 3

It's a busy night for room service. Use the clues provided to match up the food, drink, and room numbers for the hotel's guests on the third floor.

		Entree					Drink			
		Chicken Teriyaki	Fried Chicken	Parmesan Sirloin	Roast Veg Risotto	Vegetarian Burger	Diet Cola	Hard Cider	Passionfruit Seltzer	Root Beer	White Wine
Room Number	301										
	302										
	303										
	304										
	305										
Drink	Diet Cola										
	Hard Cider										
	Passionfruit Seltzer										
	Root Beer										
	White Wine										

Room 302 ordered one of the chicken dishes, and the other chicken dish was ordered along with a root beer.

The room that ordered the hard cider is directly across the hall from the room that ordered the veggie burger.

The passionfruit seltzer was ordered by the room directly across the hall from the room that ordered the fried chicken.

The rooms that ordered root beer and the veggie burger are both on the same side of the hall.

Room 303 ordered either the parmesan sirloin or the passionfruit seltzer, but did not order both.

The passionfruit seltzer was ordered by a room next to the one that ordered risotto.

Room 301 ordered a diet cola and a vegetarian dish.

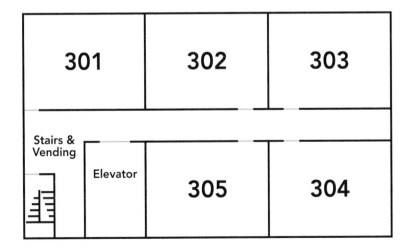

Kakuro 4

Fill the grid with digits 1 through 9 so that each continuous section of row or column contains no repeated digits, and sums to the total provided at the top or left of the section.

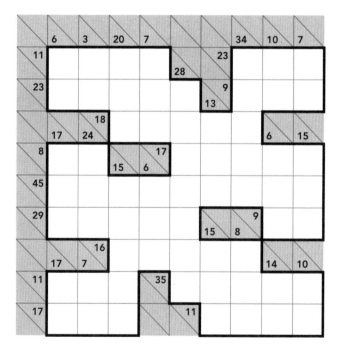

Symbol Sums 5

The sums of five combinations of symbols have been provided.
What is the value of each individual symbol?

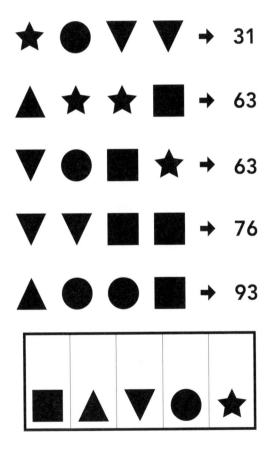

Transit Map 4

Use the clues to fill the bus route with letters to form words both northbound and southbound.

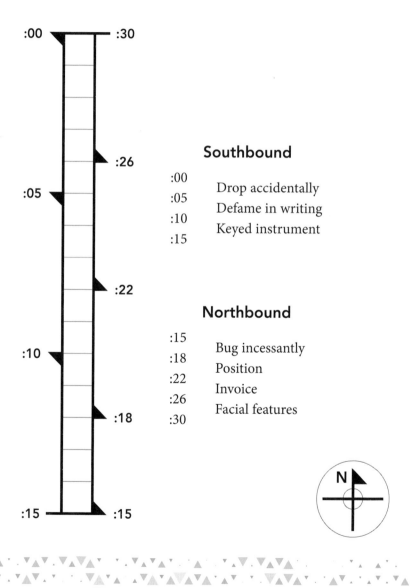

Southbound

:00
:05   Drop accidentally
:10   Defame in writing
:15   Keyed instrument

Northbound

:15
:18   Bug incessantly
:22   Position
:26   Invoice
:30   Facial features

Numcross 6

Use the provided clues to fill the grid with numbers. No entry may start with a 0.

Across

A. One-half of J across
D. A multiple of 3
F. D across × 7
G. A perfect square
H. Another multiple of 3
J. D across × G across
K. K down - 1
L. A set of odd digits that sum to 17
O. K down × 2
P. A palindrome

Down

A. Forms a sequence with N down and D across
B. M down - 1
C. Consecutive digits in descending order
D. D across × N down
E. Ounces per pint
I. C down - B down
J. J across - E down
K. One-third of M down
M. J across - H across
N. Sum of digits in J down

Rearrangement 9–10

Rearrange the letters in the phrase "MARKET FORWARD" to spell some new decor that could be bought with stock dividends.

Rearrange the letters in the phrase "TYPO BLASTER" to spell something that might be a bit overkill for applying correction fluid.

Throwing Shade 5

Shade some cells so the remaining letters in each row and column spell answers to the provided clues. Clues are sorted alphabetically by answer.

C	B	A	J	U	T	U	N	N
A	T	T	E	S	T	S	W	S
W	A	T	L	H	E	R	Y	O
U	G	I	L	F	N	Y	I	Y
B	L	E	O	E	N	D	I	D
E	A	I	F	R	O	R	T	H
I	I	C	L	O	T	U	E	E
A	P	U	T	R	E	E	S
N	M	C	O	M	E	P	L	Y

Rows

- One of the elements
- Creative disciplines
- Smoothie-maker's verb
- Spicy cuisine
- Mystery board game
- Cleaning tool
- Exams
- Possible enby pronoun
- Aesthetically displeasing

Columns

- Storage spot
- Land of premium cigars
- Nintendo handheld
- Razzle-dazzle
- Jiggly dessert
- December 31st, in short
- Pancake topping
- Camper's shelter
- Theater employee

Rows Garden 3

Using the clues provided, enter a letter into each triangle to fill the garden. Each row contains one or two entries, and each hexagonal flower contains a six-letter word wrapped around the center. It's up to you to determine where to place the starting letter and the direction of the word.

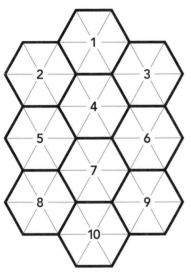

Command for a dog

Hamilton creator Miranda

Holiday song topic/Suggest

Traveler/Banana company

Unlocking items/Reusable bags

Gardening tool/Icy dwelling

Waterway/"Hey!"

Fisher's tool

Flowers

1. Praying bug
2. Connected to the web
3. Gas up
4. Firetruck feature
5. Type of primate
6. Street corn
7. Cheap cigar
8. Chips with toppings
9. Bar furniture
10. Solar system occupant

Cube Logic 4

Which of the four foldable patterns can be folded to make the cube displayed?

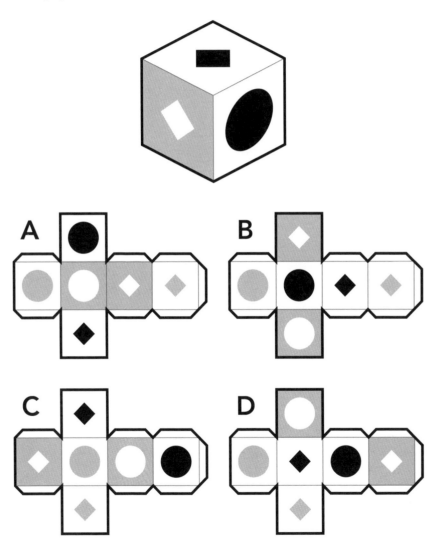

Tetra Grid 6

Drop each of the shapes into the grid in the order provided to spell ten six-letter words. Clues for the words have been provided next to the grid.

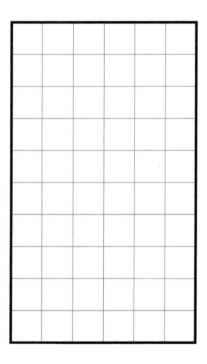

Select

Dispersed randomly

Thanksgiving centerpiece

Digestive system part

Days in some months

Breakfast pastry

All good

Diner's tool

Secretive

Change

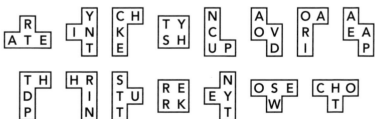

Sudoku Bites 3–4

In these two sudoku bites, fill each row, column, and thick-outlined rectangle with one of each digit 1 through 6. There are also greater-than and less-than symbols to help clue the correct digits.

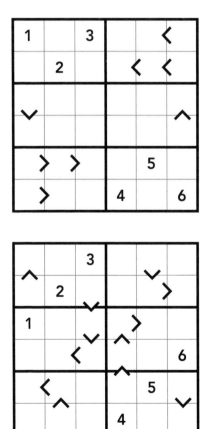

Numcross 7

Use the provided clues to fill the grid with numbers. No entry may start with a 0.

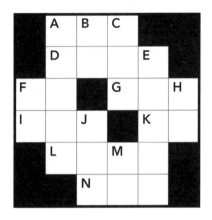

Across

A. H down × 4

D. Year of the Apollo 11 moon landing

F. Sum of the digits in D across

G. C down + 10

I. K across × 4

K. A perfect square

L. Digits that sum to F across

N. F across × 5

Down

A. F across × J down

B. F down × 3

C. A palindrome

E. Consecutive digits not in order

F. One-third of B down

H. One-half of M down

J. A across in reverse

M. K across + 1

In Memoriam 4A

Memorize the shapes shown in the grid below. When you're ready, turn the page and put your memory to the test.

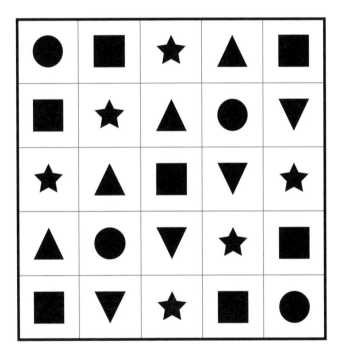

In Memoriam 4B

In the grid below, find the one row or column whose shapes are all different from the shapes in the same position on the previous page.

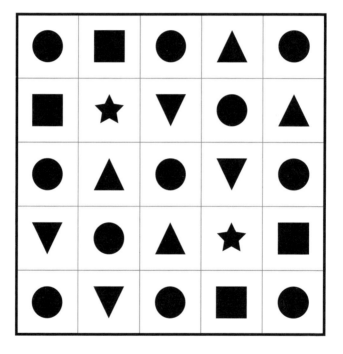

Symbol Sums 6

The sums of five combinations of symbols have been provided.
What is the value of each individual symbol?

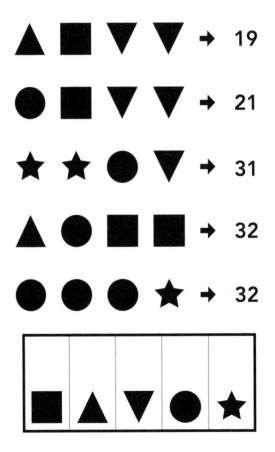

Rows Garden 4

Using the clues provided, enter a letter into each triangle to fill the garden. Each row contains one or two entries, and each hexagonal flower contains a six-letter word wrapped around the center. It's up to you to determine where to place the starting letter and the direction of the word.

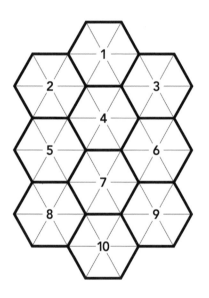

Homer's neighbor

Go back a step/Animal handler

Gut/Actress Lynch

YouTuber's journal/Huge

Written opinion/Actor Epps

Put away/"New line" keyboard key

Footwear/Metallic supplement

Miner's find

Flowers

1. Sought forgiveness
2. Collected group
3. Change a title
4. Wobbly
5. Puzzlers' achievements
6. Slogan or motto
7. Rule applied to a street
8. Photography sessions
9. Idiot
10. Some binary digits

Rearrangement 11–12

Rearrange the letters in the phrase "HELIPORT GIFT" to spell a member of the Air Force.

Rearrange the letters in the phrase "TROLL PASTRIES" to spell something more useful in a taqueria than bakery.

Throwing Shade 6

Shade some cells so the remaining letters in each row and column spell answers to the provided clues. Clues are sorted alphabetically by answer.

A	B	Z	U	Z	R	U	R	E
T	B	O	B	N	U	R	S	E
P	E	Z	R	O	M	I	T	L
P	E	O	G	U	L	L	K	L
P	A	N	E	G	U	G	L	L
P	T	P	A	N	E	E	O	E
L	E	N	N	D	L	N	O	E
E	N	N	T	E	L	T	R	K
E	L	E	N	L	E	L	K	L

Rows

- Brilliantly blue
- Extra
- Antlered beast
- Go in
- Type of bird
- Borrow
- Assembly
- Written approval
- Lower Digit

Columns

- Tree fruit
- Defeated
- Legally Blonde protagonist
- Unwell
- Unclothed
- A spirit
- Baby deliverer
- Dire
- Area

Cube Logic 5

Which of the four foldable patterns can be folded to make the cube displayed?

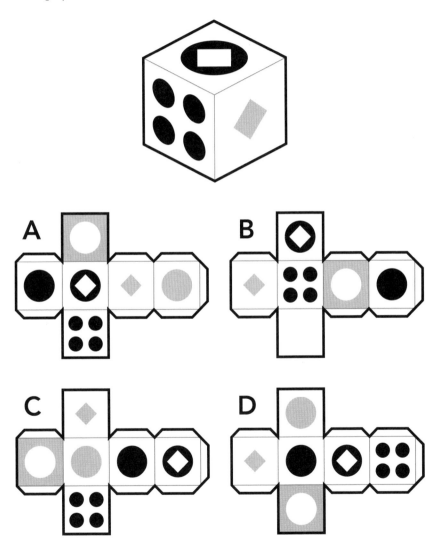

Tetra Grid 7

Drop each of the shapes into the grid in the order provided to spell ten six-letter words. Clues for the words have been provided next to the grid.

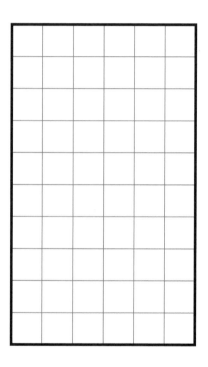

Ethereal

Garb

Golfer Palmer

Unmask

Negotiate

Measure of something

Oft-lucky ground cover

Curry paste ingredient

Dog from Peanuts

Centerpoint

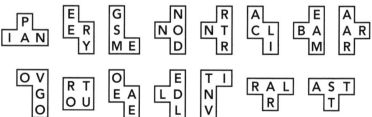

Numcross 8

Use the provided clues to fill the grid with numbers. No entry may start with a 0.

A	B	C		D	E
F				G	
		H	I		
	J				
K			L	M	N
O			P		

Across

A.   E down × N down
D.   One-half of G across
F.   A palindrome
G.   A perfect square
H.   D down × 2
J.   D across × N down
K.   A down × 3
L.   M down × 7
O.   Another perfect square
P.   Consecutive digits in descending order

Down

A.   A factor of L across
B.   G across + O across
C.   Digits that sum to E down
D.   Degrees in a circle
E.   Product of the digits in P across
I.   E down × F across
J.   D down - E down
K.   O across in reverse
M.   One-seventh of L across
N.   One-half of E down

Story Logic 4

A group of podcasts are doing a big live stream event on an upcoming Saturday. Use the clues to determine the schedule including times for each podcast, their show topic, and what they're giving away for the big event.

		BROmaha Nebraska	Country Chick Science	The Investiga-Twins	It's Halloween Somewhere	Bluetooth Earbuds	Cat Furniture	Meal Kit Plan	RFID-Block Wallet	Ghost Sightings	Haunted Prisons	Lake Monsters	Lunar Anomalies
		Podcast				**Giveaway**				**Topic**			
Time	5:00 PM												
	6:20 PM												
	7:40 PM												
	9:00 PM												
Topic	Ghost Sightings												
	Haunted Prisons												
	Lake Monsters												
	Lunar Anomalies												
Giveaway	Bluetooth Earbuds												
	Cat Furniture												
	Meal Kit Plan												
	RFID-Block Wallet												

Neither the first nor the last podcast is giving away the meal kit plan.

The show giving away cat furniture is going between the one about ghost sightings and Country Chick Science.

It's Halloween Somewhere is scheduled to be the last podcast of the night.

BROmaha Nebraska is going on after the show covering lunar anomalies but before the one giving away the RFID-block wallet.

The show covering lake monsters is going right before The Investiga-Twins.

BROmaha Nebraska and Country Chick Science are not back-to-back in the schedule.

The Investiga-Twins are covering either lunar anomalies or ghost sightings.

Kakuro 5

Fill the grid with digits 1 through 9 so that each continuous section of row or column contains no repeated digits, and sums to the total provided at the top or left of the section.

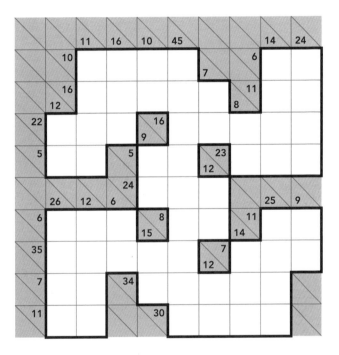

Cube Logic 6

Which of the four foldable patterns can be folded to make the cube displayed?

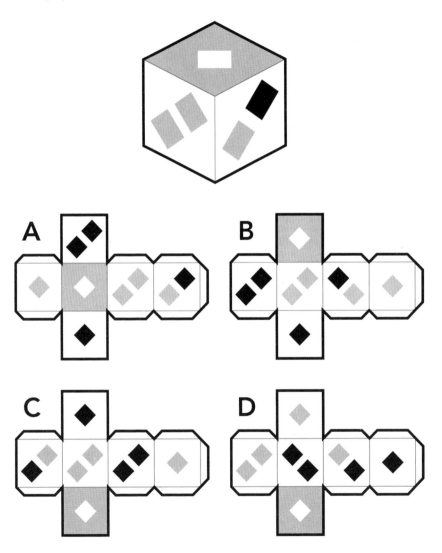

Symbol Sums 7

The sums of five combinations of symbols have been provided. What is the value of each individual symbol?

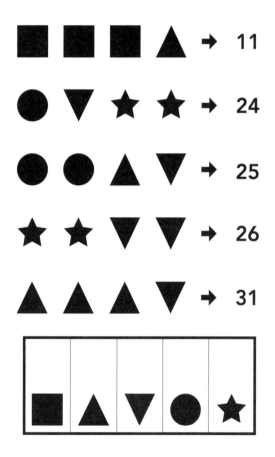

Rearrangement 13–14

Rearrange the letters in the phrase "A REAL CLASSMATE" to spell an ice cream flavor so good, you'd make up an imaginary friend to get an extra bowl of it.

Rearrange the letters in the phrase "PAINLESS SOON" to spell some musical sessions that will get better over time.

Sudoku Bites 5–6

In these two sudoku bites, fill each row, column, and thick-outlined rectangle with one of each digit 1 through 6. Digits placed in the dash-outlined cages must sum to the provided total.

Rebus Deli 5–6

What tasty morsels are clued by the pictures?

HOLA
ME LLAMO

SAUCE

		1	2	3	4	5
6	7	8	9	10	11	12
13 (HOT FUDGE)	14	15	16	17	18	19
20	21	22	23	24	25	26
27	28	29	30			

Numcross 9

Use the provided clues to fill the grid with numbers. No entry may start with a 0.

A	B		C	D	E
F			G		
H		I			
		J		K	L
M	N			O	
P				Q	

Across

A. Sum of all digits in the solution to this puzzle

C. G across × 4

F. A perfect square

G. A power of two

H. Comprised of the digits in D down

J. A palindrome

M. Digits that sum to D down

O. D down × 6

P. Q across × 2

Q. E down × 2

Down

A. Digits that sum to a prime number

B. Another palindrome

C. D down × L down

D. A factor of B down

E. Number of unshaded squares in this puzzle

I. Another palindrome

K. F across × M down

L. N down × 6

M. D down - 1

N. O across – 1

Throwing Shade 7

Shade some cells so the remaining letters in each row and column spell answers to the provided clues. Clues are sorted alphabetically by answer.

S	K	M	O	D	C	F	K	K
U	A	U	T	R	H	R	F	A
R	D	I	U	C	E	T	T	H
U	R	I	C	H	D	E	F	A
T	I	D	C	E	A	N	K	A
M	Y	A	R	I	T	U	R	Y
S	I	S	H	A	D	R	E	A
M	P	S	H	P	I	T	T	A
T	K	A	N	T	A	N	K	K

Rows

- Air tunnel
- Concept
- Daytime talk host
- A type of flatbread
- Wealthy
- Give, in part
- Worker's garb
- Storage vessel
- "Weird Al" movie

Columns

- Swindle
- Green "pet" covering
- Coffee prep method
- Worry
- Narrow boat
- Legendary king
- Exclamation of pain
- Total
- Change direction

Tetra Grid 8

Drop each of the shapes into the grid in the order provided to spell ten six-letter words. Clues for the words have been provided next to the grid.

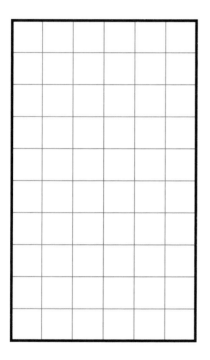

European country

Hockey position

Agree to

Brawn

Streaming platform

Origin

Geographical area

Difficult

Leave

Casino employee

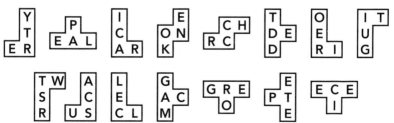

Rearrangement 15–16

Rearrange the letters in the phrase "WANTING CARE" to spell a tool used to look after plants in need of some care.

Rearrange the letters in the phrase "OUR GAZERS" to spell a feature of some energy drinks that late-night stargazers might appreciate.

Rebus Deli 7–8

What tasty morsels are clued by the pictures?

W   W **E**   W

Cube Logic 7

Which of the four foldable patterns can be folded to make the cube displayed?

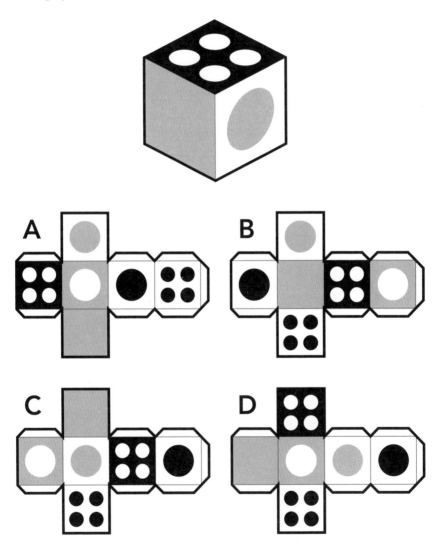

Rows Garden 5

Using the clues provided, enter a letter into each triangle to fill the garden. Each row contains one or two entries, and each hexagonal flower contains a six-letter word wrapped around the center. It's up to you to determine where to place the starting letter and the direction of the word.

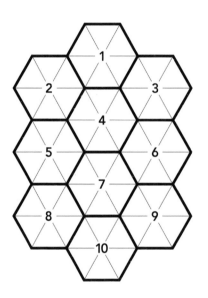

Tombstone inscription

Designer Jacobs / Market booth

Hopeless / Measure of land

Holiday visitor / Good

Try again / Swam

Climate systems / Desiccated

Vocalize music / Measuring device

Nada

Flowers

1.	Actor's directives	6.	Make a choice
2.	Carry on aimlessly	7.	One lacking courage
3.	Talk radio participant	8.	Disappear
4.	Japanese sword	9.	Depended
5.	Woodworking machine	10.	Court outcome

Kakuro 6

Fill the grid with digits 1 through 9 so that each continuous section of row or column contains no repeated digits, and sums to the total provided at the top or left of the section.

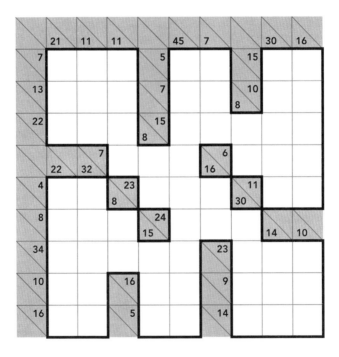

Cube Logic 8

Which two of the six foldable patterns can be folded to make the same cube?

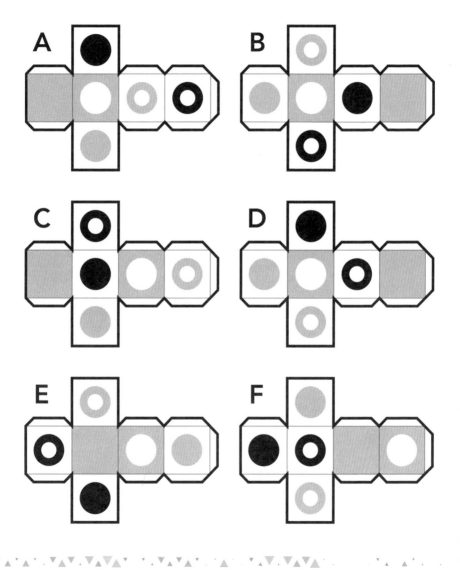

Symbol Sums 8

The sums of five combinations of symbols have been provided.
What is the value of each individual symbol?

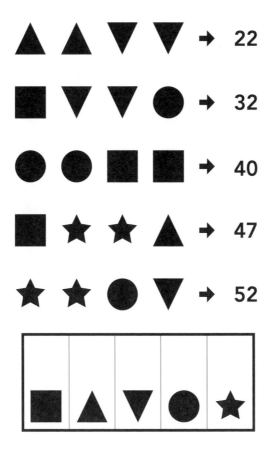

Numcross 10

Use the provided clues to fill the grid with numbers. No entry may start with a 0.

A	B	C		D	E	F		G	H
I				J				K	
L			M			N	O		
P			Q		R		S		
T		U			V	W			
		X		Y		Z		AA	BB
CC	DD			EE	FF			GG	
HH			II		JJ			KK	
LL			MM	NN			OO		
PP			QQ				RR		

Across

A.   A power of two

D.   P across × PP across

G.   KK across + PP across

I.   A palindrome

J.   Odd digits that sum to PP across

K.   GG across + KK across

L.   P across + KK across

M.   One-third of NN down

N.   CC across × 2

P.   KK across + 1

Q.   L across × 4

S.   NN down + RR across

T.   F down × PP across

V.   C down × PP across

X.   One-third of W down

Z.   G down - 1

CC.   Another palindrome

EE.   NN down × 9

GG.   A perfect square

HH.   D down × 2

JJ.   One-half of K across

KK.   Sum of the digits in BB down

LL.   K across + KK across

MM.   QQ across - 8

OO.   QQ across in reverse

PP.   Sum of the digits in QQ across

QQ.   One-fourth of H down

RR.   G across × 8

Down

A.   Digits sum to PP across

B.   Digits multiply to KK across

C.   NN down - 7

D.   Digits sum to PP across

E.   K across + 1

F.   E down × 3

G.   Another palindrome

H.   BB down / GG across

M.   Another palindrome

O.   Z across in reverse

R.   Another perfect square

U.   An anagram of HH across

W.   F down + FF down

Y.   E down + G across

AA.   Consecutive digits not in order

BB.   Contains one of each even digit

CC.   Digits that sum to GG across

DD.   A palindrome

FF.   Odd digits that sum to JJ across

II.   Consecutive digits in ascending order

NN.   JJ across × 5

OO.   K across × 2

Throwing Shade 8

Shade some cells so the remaining letters in each row and column spell answers to the provided clues. Clues are sorted alphabetically by answer.

T	A	P	S	W	A	M	E	P
R	H	I	M	H	D	S	D	L
E	I	N	O	E	D	E	U	A
B	B	V	H	K	U	S	C	K
A	Y	O	C	H	E	I	R	E
I	B	E	H	E	T	X	O	T
M	B	T	H	N	S	I	D	N
B	B	E	A	Y	O	S	U	T
E	A	R	U	M	S	T	O	E

Rows	**Columns**
• Marshland	• Dancing Queen singers
• Dollar	• Pairs
• Where the sun rises	• Color of plain fabric
• Mountain goat	• Leave
• Singular point	• "Yo!"
• Earthy yellow	• Barbie's male friend
• Edge	• Chocolate/coffee combo
• Pre-DVD format	• Type of wine
• Svelte	• Group

Tetra Grid 9

Drop each of the shapes into the grid in the order provided to spell ten six-letter words. Clues for the words have been provided next to the grid.

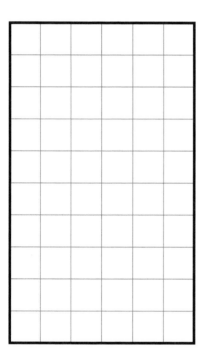

Meltable decor

Spring holiday

Building material

Proofreader

Get down?

Shore up

On the same page

Item from an ATM

Iconic horror hostess

Mythical fire-breather

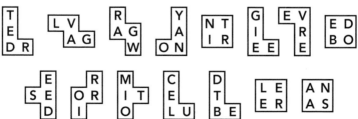

Cube Logic 9

Which two of the six foldable patterns can be folded to make the same cube?

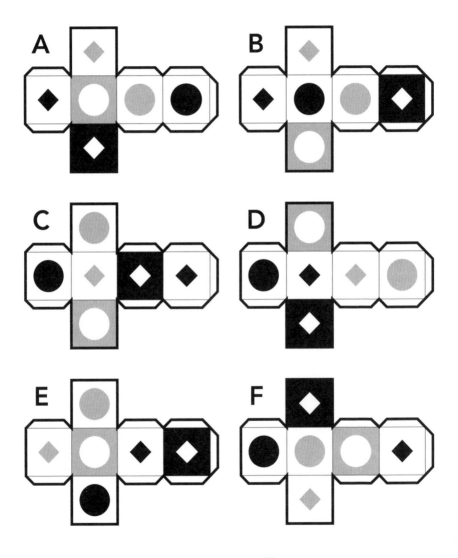

Rearrangement 17–18

Rearrange the letters in the phrase "TURNIP DEBACLE" to spell a word that might describe a turnip debacle.

Rearrange the letters in the phrase "BAKED CHARITY" to spell a baked good every kid deserves once a year.

Story Logic 5

Four customers have arrived for curbside pickup of their grocery orders. Most of the items are bagged and ready to go; you only need to match the customer's vehicle with their order number, frozen item, and meat counter item.

		Vehicle				Meat Counter				Frozen			
		Blue Truck	Orange Car	Red Car	Red SUV	Bacon	Pork Loin	Sausage Links	Skirt Steak	Blueberries	Ice Cream	Orange Juice	Personal Pizza
Order #	1743												
	1749												
	1760												
	1773												
Frozen	Blueberries												
	Ice Cream												
	Orange Juice												
	Personal Pizza												
Meat Counter	Bacon												
	Pork Loin												
	Sausage Links												
	Skirt Steak												

The orders are numbered sequentially as placed.

The customers in the two cars ordered the bacon and skirt steak orders.

The customer who ordered frozen blueberries also ordered either bacon or skirt steak from the meat counter.

The orange car's order came in after the order that included skirt steak.

The personal pizza and sausage links are for the same order.

The red SUV's order came in before the red car's order.

The customer in the blue truck ordered either bacon or sausage links.

The blueberries and the ice cream were ordered by the two customers with red vehicles.

Order 1749 includes either personal pizza or pork loin but not both.

The blue truck did not place the earliest order of the set.

Symbol Sums 9

The sums of five combinations of symbols have been provided.
What is the value of each individual symbol?

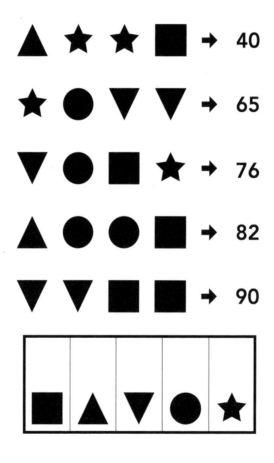

Sudoku Bites 7–8

In these two sudoku bites, fill each row, column, and thick-outlined rectangle with one of each digit 1 through 6. The clues in these puzzles function the same as in the previous bites.

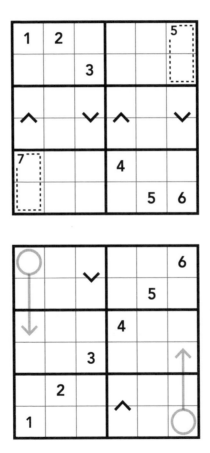

Rebus Deli 9–10

What tasty morsels are clued by the pictures?

NOW 1/3 MORE!

EGG SAL

New and improved formula.
Find it in your grocer's
freezer section.

Rearrangement 19–20

Rearrange the letters in the phrase "MODERN TRUTHS" to spell something that modern weather forecasting equipment can detect with great accuracy.

Rearrange the letters in the phrase "CRAP INTELLECT" to spell a utility company's facility that takes brainpower to build and operate.

Numcross 11

Use the provided clues to fill the grid with numbers. No entry may start with a 0.

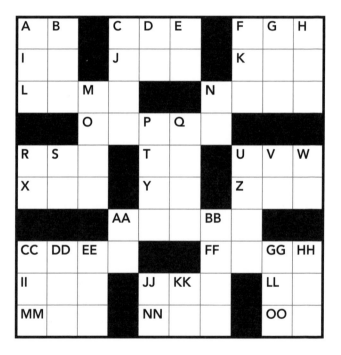

Across

A.   One-half of W down

C.   E down squared

F.   CC down × 2

I.   JJ down + 1

J.   R down × 9

K.   G down + 2

L.   Digits that sum to 15

N.   Year the Mayan calendar ended

O.   Consecutive digits in descending order

R.   A across × E down

T.   KK down - 5

U.   OO across × 6

X.   MM across × 3

Y.   OO across × 3

Z.   E down × LL across

AA.   Contains one of each even digit

CC.   K across × 5

FF.   N across + 999

II.   A multiple of D down

JJ.   JJ down squared

LL.   KK down - I across

MM.   One-third of X across

NN.   D down × E down

OO.   JJ down in reverse

Down

A.   MM across + JJ down

B.   E down × OO across

C.   G down × 3

D.   V down - 2

E.   JJ down - 1

F.   DD down × 2

G.   JJ across in reverse

H.   Digits that sum to E down

M.   AA across / N down

N.   OO across - 1

P.   Q down × 2

Q.   An anagram of M down

R.   I across × 3

S.   D down in reverse

U.   D down × S down

V.   A perfect cube

W.   Another perfect cube

AA.   W down + 1

BB.   Consecutive digits in ascending order

CC.   I across × OO across

DD.   U across + JJ across

EE.   Digits that sum to I across

GG.   E down × JJ down

HH.   A palindrome

JJ.   D down - I across

KK.   S down – 5

Symbol Sums 10

The sums of five combinations of symbols have been provided. What is the value of each individual symbol?

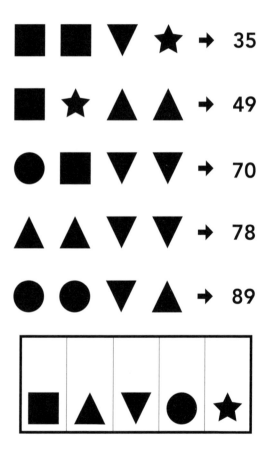

Rows Garden 6

Using the clues provided, enter a letter into each triangle to fill the garden. Each row contains one or two entries, and each hexagonal flower contains a six-letter word wrapped around the center. It's up to you to determine where to place the starting letter and the direction of the word.

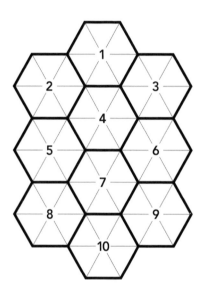

Male child

Unpleasant sound / Wheat cereal

Aquatic plant / Craft with yarn

Word or phrase / Lukewarm

Cheat in pinball / Fiber product

Dr. Who baddie / Cheese product

Basic seasoning / Light up

Curve

Flowers

1. School plan
2. Moisturizer
3. Limited
4. Old-timey gun
5. Batch of kittens
6. Little or big star pattern
7. Sauce sachet
8. Large Texas city
9. Wrecked
10. Laundry additive

Cube Logic 10

Which two of the six foldable patterns can be folded to make the same cube?

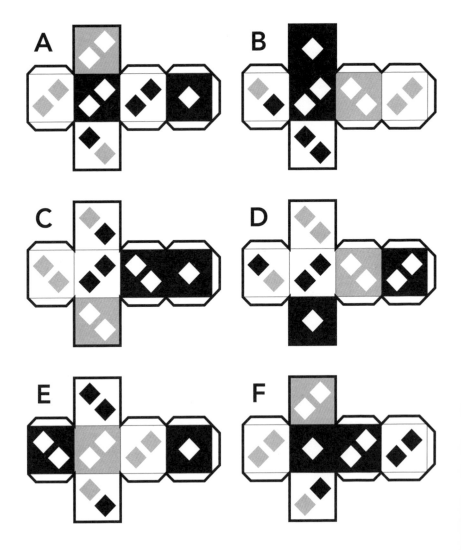

Answer Keys

Cube Logic

1:    Pattern A
2:    Pattern D
3:    Pattern B
4:    Pattern B
5:    Pattern A
6:    Pattern C
7:    Pattern C
8:    Patterns C and D
9:    Patterns A and F
10:   Patterns B and C

In Memoriam 1

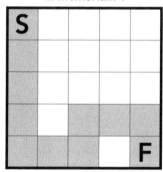

In Memoriam 2

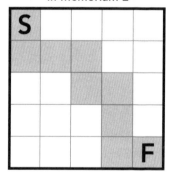

In Memoriam 3

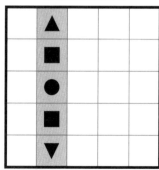

In Memoriam 4

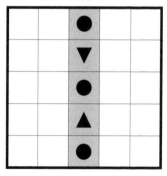

Kakuro 1

```
■  7 8 9 5 ■  4 9
■  1 4 2 8 3 ■  2 8
1 5 ■ ■ ■  2 3 1 6
3 2 1 ■  2 1 4 ■ ■
6 3 2 1 8 9 7 5 4
■  3 2 9 ■  9 2 1
8 9 7 3 ■ ■  1 3
6 1 ■  4 1 2 6 3 ■
9 7 ■  7 6 9 8 ■
```

Kakuro 2

```
3 9 ■  3 1 2 ■ ■
1 2 ■  9 7 8 6 5 ■
2 3 1 4 ■  9 3 2 1
■  2 8 9 7 ■  3 5
■  3 4 7 8 5 9 6 ■
8 7 ■  2 3 1 6 ■ ■
5 2 3 1 ■  4 8 2 1
■  1 4 6 2 3 ■  1 3
■ ■  5 1 6 ■  4 5
```

Kakuro 3

```
9 2 1 ■  6 7 9 8 ■
8 4 2 ■  2 1 4 5 3
6 1 ■  9 8 6 ■  9 2
■  9 2 8 1 ■  6 4 1
■  5 7 9 6 8 ■ ■
4 2 1 ■  5 8 9 7 ■
6 1 ■  8 7 9 ■  9 8
9 8 3 7 4 ■  1 4 2
■  9 1 2 3 ■  9 8 1
```

Kakuro 4

```
5 1 3 2 ■ ■  9 8 6
1 2 9 4 7 ■  6 2 1
■  8 1 2 3 4 ■ ■
1 7 ■  1 4 7 2 3
7 9 2 1 5 6 8 3 4
9 8 5 3 4 ■ ■  1 8
■  4 2 3 6 1 ■ ■
8 2 1 ■  6 8 5 9 7
9 5 3 ■  1 2 5 3
```

Kakuro 5

```
■  2 3 4 1 ■ ■  2 4
■  3 4 6 2 1 ■  3 8
8 5 9 ■  4 6 2 1 3
4 1 ■  2 3 ■  6 8 9
■ ■  7 8 9 ■ ■ ■
3 2 1 ■  5 3 ■  6 5
9 6 5 8 7 ■  1 2 4
6 1 ■  7 9 4 6 8 ■
8 3 ■ ■  6 8 7 9 ■
```

Kakuro 6

```
4 1 2 ■  1 4 ■  9 6
8 2 3 ■  5 2 ■  8 2
9 8 5 ■  2 1 5 4 3
■ ■  1 2 4 ■  3 2 1
1 3 ■  6 8 9 ■  7 4
2 5 1 ■  9 7 8 ■ ■
9 8 7 4 6 ■  9 8 6
3 7 ■  9 7 ■  6 2 1
7 9 ■  2 3 ■  7 4 3
```

Numcross 1

```
8 1 5 ■ 5 1
1 6 2 ■ 7 0
■ 5 1 5 1
2 8 2 4 ■
7 9 ■ 1 2 1
2 5 ■ 2 3 7
```

Numcross 2

```
3 5 ■ 5 5 5
6 9 ■ 2 3 4
1 0 2 4 ■
■ 6 6 9 2
1 2 2 ■ 7 0
8 3 3 ■ 2 7
```

Numcross 3

```
3 1 2 ■ 1 1
1 6 0 ■ 6 8
■ 1 6 9 5
1 7 3 5 ■
2 8 ■ 3 4 1
4 9 ■ 4 0 3
```

Numcross 4

```
3 6 ■ 2 8 9
1 7 ■ 4 0 5
1 8 1 8 ■
■ 1 8 3 5
1 9 1 ■ 2 2
1 0 1 ■ 1 8
```

Numcross 5

```
■ 4 2 1 ■
■ 3 7 9 1 5
3 6 ■ 1 3 5
8 5 1 ■ 9 9
2 7 2 2 7
■ 9 5 5
```

Numcross 6

```
3 7 8 ■ 2 1
1 4 7 ■ 3 6
■ 6 8 1 ■
■ 7 5 6 ■
2 4 ■ 9 7 1
5 0 ■ 1 5 1
```

Numcross 7

```
■ 1 6 4
1 9 6 9
2 5 ■ 4 7 4
3 2 4 ■ 8 1
■ 5 6 8 6
■ 1 2 5
```

Numcross 8

```
2 8 8 ■ 3 2
1 0 1 ■ 6 4
■ 7 2 0
■ 3 8 4
6 3 ■ 2 3 1
1 6 ■ 4 3 2
```

Numcross 9

```
9 2 ■ 5 1 2
2 5 ■ 1 2 8
2 2 2 1 ■
■ 4 2 2 4
1 7 4 ■ 7 2
1 1 2 ■ 5 6
```

Numcross 10

```
1 2 8 ■ 2 3 1 ■ 3 1
3 5 3 ■ 3 7 1 ■ 3 6
4 1 ■ 3 0 ■ 1 2 3 2
2 1 ■ 1 6 4 ■ 3 3 8
1 2 2 1 ■ 9 1 3 ■
■ 4 3 6 ■ 3 3 3 2
6 1 6 ■ 8 1 0 ■ 1 6
4 6 1 2 ■ 1 8 ■ 2 0
5 6 ■ 3 9 9 ■ 7 0 4
1 1 ■ 4 0 7 ■ 2 4 8
```

Numcross 11

```
3 2 ■ 1 2 1 ■ 5 4 6
1 3 ■ 3 5 1 ■ 4 4 3
9 1 3 2 ■ 2 0 1 2
■ 4 3 2 1 0 ■
3 5 2 ■ 4 2 ■ 1 2 6
9 2 1 ■ 6 3 ■ 3 7 4
■ 6 8 4 2 0 ■
2 2 1 5 ■ 3 0 1 1
7 7 5 ■ 1 4 4 ■ 3 4
3 0 7 ■ 2 7 5 ■ 2 1
```

Rearrangement

1: DIY Projects
2: Cocktail Party
3: Hollywood California
4: Ceiling Fans
5: Windshield Wipers
6: Surge Protectors
7: Toothpaste Tube
8: Submarines
9: Framed Artwork
10: Spray Bottle
11: Fighter Pilot
12: Tortilla Press
13: Sea Salt Caramel
14: Piano Lessons
15: Watering Can
16: Zero Sugar
17: Unpredictable
18: Birthday Cake
19: Thunderstorm
20: Electric Plant

Rebus Deli

1: Everything Bagel
2: Green Onions
3: Meatball Sub
4: Lemonade
5: Soy Sauce
6: Hot Fudge Sundae
7: White Wine
8: Spiral Sliced Ham
9: Egg Salad
10: Cold Brew

Rows Garden 1

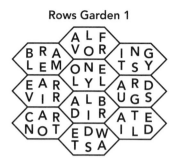

Rows Garden 2

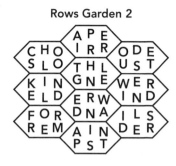

Rows Garden 3

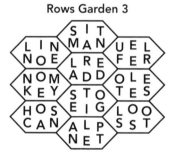

Rows Garden 4

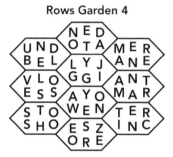

Rows Garden 5

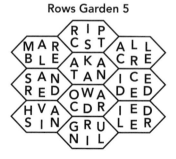

Rows Garden 6

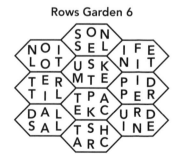

Story Logic 1

February in Denton: Cowboy Carter vs Terrible Terry.

April in Mineral Wells: Danny B vs Quick Shot Sal.

June in Waco: Fly Frank Smith vs Randy Willis.

August in Abilene: Easy Gary Easton vs Smooth Stunta.

Story Logic 2

Linda has the blue car that needs brake service.

Mark has the blue SUV that needs its tires rotated.

Neisha has the red SUV that needs its battery replaced.

Olly has the yellow car that needs the AC diagnosed/fixed.

Pal has the green van that needs an oil change.

Story Logic 3

Room 301 ordered Roast Veg Risotto and Diet Cola.

Room 302 ordered Chicken Teriyaki and Passionfruit Seltzer.

Room 303 ordered Parmesan Sirloin and Hard Cider.

Room 304 ordered a Veggie Burger and White Wine.

Room 305 ordered Fried Chicken and Root Beer.

Story Logic 4

At 5:00 p.m., Country Chick Science did an episode on lake monsters and gave away bluetooth earbuds.

At 6:20 p.m., The Investiga-Twins did an episode about lunar anomalies and gave away cat furniture.

At 7:40 p.m., BROmaha Nebraska did an episode on ghost sightings and gave away a meal kit plan.

At 9:00 p.m., It's Halloween Somewhere did an episode about haunted prisons and gave away an RFID-block wallet.

Story Logic 5

Order number 1743, which requires ice cream and pork loin, is for the red SUV.

Order number 1749, which requires personal pizza and sausage links, is for the blue truck.

Order number 1760, which requires frozen blueberries and skirt steak, is for the red car.

Order number 1773, which requires orange juice concentrate and bacon, is for the orange car.

Sudoku Bites 1

6	3	2	1	4	5
5	4	1	3	2	6
1	2	5	4	6	3
4	6	3	5	1	2
2	5	4	6	3	1
3	1	6	2	5	4

Sudoku Bites 2

3	5	2	4	6	1
1	4	6	2	3	5
4	3	1	6	5	2
2	6	5	1	4	3
5	2	4	3	1	6
6	1	3	5	2	4

Sudoku Bites 3

1	5	3	6	2	4
4	2	6	1	3	5
3	6	5	2	4	1
2	1	4	5	6	3
6	4	1	3	5	2
5	3	2	4	1	6

Sudoku Bites 4

4	1	3	2	6	5
5	2	6	1	4	3
1	6	5	3	2	4
2	3	4	5	1	6
3	4	1	6	5	2
6	5	2	4	3	1

Sudoku Bites 5

5	1	3	2	4	6
4	6	2	1	5	3
6	5	1	3	2	4
3	2	4	6	1	5
2	4	6	5	3	1
1	3	5	4	6	2

Sudoku Bites 6

4	3	6	1	2	5
2	5	1	3	6	4
1	6	4	2	5	3
5	2	3	4	1	6
3	1	5	6	4	2
6	4	2	5	3	1

Sudoku Bites 7

1	2	5	3	6	4
6	4	3	5	2	1
3	1	6	2	4	5
4	5	2	6	1	3
5	6	1	4	3	2
2	3	4	1	5	6

Sudoku Bites 8

5	4	2	3	1	6
3	6	1	2	5	4
2	5	6	4	3	1
4	1	3	5	6	2
6	2	5	1	4	3
1	3	4	6	2	5

Symbol Sums 1

Symbol Sums 2

Symbol Sums 3

Symbol Sums 4

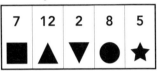

Symbol Sums 5

Symbol Sums 6

Symbol Sums 7

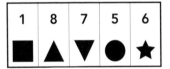

Symbol Sums 8

Symbol Sums 9

Symbol Sums 10

Tetra Grid 1

```
A S S E S S
T R A S H Y
R E A S O N
D E C E N T
B L A N K S
B O S T O N
D I V I D E
G R E A S E
D E A L E R
C E N S U S
```

Tetra Grid 2

```
A F F E C T
F L I G H T
C A M P E R
I S S U E D
S H R I N E
B L I N D S
F I N G E R
A G E N D A
C H R O M E
A T R I U M
```

Tetra Grid 3

```
R E T U R N
S N A C K S
I C I C L E
S H R I N K
L I Q U I D
S L I D E R
P A L A C E
I D I O C Y
L A W Y E R
A S L E E P
```

Tetra Grid 4

```
A L M O N D
S T R I P E
C H A P E L
T E M P L E
M O S A I C
S L I G H T
B A N A N A
R E V E R B
G R A V E L
D O N G L E
```

Tetra Grid 5

```
S T R U C K
P R A I S E
M A I D E N
E D I B L E
N I B B L E
S T A B L E
M I N T E D
D O Z E N S
U N D E A D
I S L A N D
```

Tetra Grid 6

```
C H O O S E
S T R E W N
T U R K E Y
T H R O A T
T H I R T Y
D A N I S H
P E A C H Y
N A P K I N
C O V E R T
U P D A T E
```

Tetra Grid 7

```
A S T R A L
A T T I R E
A R N O L D
R E V E A L
B A R T E R
A M O U N T
C L O V E R
G I N G E R
S N O O P Y
M E D I A N
```

Tetra Grid 8

```
G R E E C E
G O A L I E
A C C E P T
M U S C L E
T W I T C H
S O U R C E
R E G I O N
T R I C K Y
D E P A R T
D E A L E R
```

Tetra Grid 9

```
C A N D L E
E A S T E R
L U M B E R
E D I T O R
B O O G I E
R E V I S E
A G R E E D
T W E N T Y
E L V I R A
D R A G O N
```

The Tetra Grid puzzles are where you'll find the Word Search words.

Throwing Shade 1

Throwing Shade 2

Throwing Shade 3

Throwing Shade 4

Throwing Shade 5

Throwing Shade 6

Throwing Shade 7

Throwing Shade 8

Transit Map 1

Southbound		Northbound	
:00	DROWSY	:15	MEGA
:06	ALPACA	:19	CAP
:12	GEM	:22	LAYS
:15		:26	WORD
		:30	

Transit Map 2

Southbound		Northbound	
:00	KNITS	:15	LIAR
:05	IGLOO	:19	FOOL
:10	FRAIL	:23	GIST
:15		:27	INK
		:30	

Transit Map 3

Southbound		Northbound	
:00	SPIDER	:15	ANDREW
:06	ANSWER	:21	SNARE
:12	DNA	:26	DIPS
:15		:30	

Transit Map 4

Southbound		Northbound	
:00	SPILL	:15	NAG
:05	LIBEL	:18	ROLE
:10	ORGAN	:22	BILL
:15		:26	LIPS
		:30	

Thank you for solving!

**This book is dedicated to my cats,
and my good friends and cat-sitters,
John & Olivia Krull**

Exercise Your Mind at American Mensa

At American Mensa, we love puzzles. In fact, we have events—large and small—centered around games and puzzles.

Of course, with tens of thousands of members and growing, we're much more than that, with members aged 2 to 102 and from all walks of life. Our one shared trait might be one you share too: high intelligence, measured in the top 2 percent of the general public in a standardized test.

Get-togethers with other Mensans—from small pizza nights up to larger events like our annual Mind Games—are always stimulating and fun. Roughly 130 Special Interest Groups (we call them SIGs) offer the best of the real and virtual worlds. Highlighting the Mensa newsstand is our award-winning magazine, *Mensa Bulletin*, which stimulates the curious mind with unique features that add perspective to our fast-paced world.

And then there are the practical benefits of membership, such as exclusive offers through our partners and member discounts on magazine subscriptions, online shopping, and financial services.

Find out how to qualify or take our practice test at americanmensa.org/join. Use code TWISTERS to take the Mensa Practice Test for just $1.